Mr. Dryden

Albion and Albanius: An Opera

Mr. Dryden

Albion and Albanius: An Opera

ISBN/EAN: 9783742842190

Manufactured in Europe, USA, Canada, Australia, Japa

Cover: Foto ©Andreas Hilbeck / pixelio.de

Manufactured and distributed by brebook publishing software
(www.brebook.com)

Mr. Dryden

Albion and Albanius: An Opera

ALBION
AND
ALBANIUS:
AN
OPERA.

Perform'd at the QUEENS Theatre
in *Dorset*-Garden.

Written by Mr. Dryden.

Discite Justitiam moniti, & non temnere Divos. Virg.

LONDON,

Printed for *Jacob Tonson,* at the *Judge's Head*
in *Chancery-Lane,* near *Fleet-Street.* 1691.

THE
PREFACE.

IF Wit has truly been defin'd a Propriety of Thoughts and Words, then that Definition will extend to all sorts of Poetry ; and amongst the rest, to this present Entertainment of an *Opera*. Propriety of Thought is that Fancy which arises naturally from the Subject, or which the Poet adapts to it. Propriety of Words, is the cloathing of those Thoughts with such Expressions, as are naturally proper to them : And from both these, if they are judiciously perform'd, the delight of Poetry results. An *Opera* is a Poetical Tale, or Fiction, represented by Vocal and Istrumental Musick, adorn'd with Scenes, Machines, and Dancing. The suppos'd Persons of this Musical *Drama*, are generally supernatural, as Gods, and Goddesses, and Heroes, which at least are descended from them, and are in due time, to be adopted into their Number. The Subject therefore being extended beyond the Limits of Humane Nature, admits of that sort of marvellous and surprizing Conduct, which is rejected in other Plays. Humane Impossibilties are to be receiv'd, as they are in Faith ; because where Gods are introduc'd, a Supreme Power is to be understood, and second Causes are out of doors : Yet Propriety is to be observ'd even here. The Gods are all to manage their peculiar Provinces ; and what was attributed by the Heathens to one Power, ought not to be perform'd by any other. *Phœbus* must foretel, *Mercury* must charm with his *Caduceus*, and *Juno* must reconcile the Quarrels of the Marriage-Bed. To conclude, they must all act according to their distinct and peculiar Characters. If the Persons represented were to speak upon the Stage, it wou'd follow of necessity, That the Expressions should be Lofty, Figurative, and Majestical : But the Nature of an *Opera* denies the frequent use of those

Poetical

Poetical Ornaments: For Vocal Mufick, though it often admits a Loftinefs of Sound; yet always exacts an harmonious Sweetnefs: or to diſtinguiſh yet more juſtly, The recitative Part of the *Opera* requires a more Mafculine Beauty of Expreſſion and Sound : The other, which (for want of a proper Engliſh Word) I muſt call *The Songiſh Part*, muſt abound in the Softnefs and Variety of Numbers ; its principal Intention, being to pleafe the Hearing, rather than to gratifie the Underſtanding. It appears indeed prepoſterous at firſt fight, That Rhime, on any confideration ſhould take place of Rcafon. But in order to refolve the Probleme, this fundamental Propofition muſt be fetled, That the firſt Inventors of any Art or Science, provided they have brought it to perfeċtion, are, in reafon, to give Laws to it; and according to their Model, all after-undertakers are to build. Thus in Epique Poetry, no Man ought to difpute the Authority of *Homer*, who gave the firſt Being to that Maſter-piece of Art, and endued it with that Form of Perfeċtion in all its Parts., that nothing was wanting to its excellency. *Virgil* therefore, and thofe very few who have fucceeded him, endeavour'd not to introduce or innovate any thing in a Defign already perfeċted, but imitated the Plan of the Inventor ; and are only fo far true Heroick Poets, as they have built on the Foundations of *Homer*. Thus *Pindar*, the Author of thofe Odes , (which are fo admirably reſtor'd by Mr. *Cowley* in our Language,) ought for ever to be the Standard of them; and we are bound according to the praċtice of *Horace* and Mr. *Cowley*, to Copy him. Now, to apply this Axiom to our prefent purpofe, whofoever undertakes the writing of an *Opera*, (which is a modern invention, though built indeed, on the Foundations of Ethnick Worſhip,) is oblig'd to imitate the Defign of the *Italians*, who have not only invented, but brought to perfeċtion, this fort of Dramatick Mufical Entertainment. I have not been able, by any fearch, to get any light either of the time, when it began, or of the firſt Author. But I have probable Reafons, which induce me to believe, that fome *Italians* having curiouſly obferv'd the Gallantries of the *Spaniſh Moors* at their *Zambra's*, or Royal Feaſts, where Mufick, Songs, and Dancing were in perfeċtion ; together with their Machines, which are ufual at their *Sortiia's*, or running at the Ring, and other Solemnities, may poffibly have refin'd upon thofe Morefque Divertifements, and produc'd this delightful Entertainment, by leaving out the warlike Part of the Caroufels, and forming a Poetical Defign for the ufe of
the

the Machines, the Songs, and Dances. But however it began,
(for this is only conjectural,) we know that for some Centuries,
the knowledge of Musick has flourish'd principally in *Italy*, the Mother of Learning and of Arts; that Poetry and Painting have been
there restor'd and so cultivated by *Italian* Masters, That all *Europe*
has been enrich'd out of their Treasury, aud the other Parts of it
in relation to those delightful Arts, are still a smuch Provincial to
Italy, as they were in the time of the *Roman* Empire. Their first
Opera's seem to have been intended for the Celebration of the Marriages of their Princes, or for the Magnificence of some general time
of Joy. Accordingly the Expences of them were from the Purse
of the Sovereign, or of the Republick, as they are still practis'd at
Venice, *Rome*, and other Places at their Carnivals. *Savoy* and *Florence* have often us'd them in their Courts, at the Weddings of their
Dukes: And at *Turin* particularly, was perform'd the *Pastor Fide*,
written by the famous *Guarini*, which is a Pastoral *Opera* made to
solemnize the Marriage of a Duke of *Savoy*. The Prologue of it has
given the Design to all the *French*; which is a Complement to the
Sovereign Power by some God or Goddesses; so that it looks no less
than a kind of Embassie from Heaven to Earth. I said in the beginning
of this Preface, that the Persons represented in *Opera's*, are generally Gods, Goddesses, and Heroes descended from them, who are
suppos'd to be their peculiar Care; which hinders not, but that
meaner Persons may sometimes gracefully be introduc'd, especially
if they have relation to those first Times, which Poets call the *Golden Age*: wherein by reason of their Innocence, those happy Mortals were suppos'd to have had a more familiar Intercourse with Superiour Beings; and therefore Shepherds might reasonably be admitted, as of all Callings, the most innocent, the most happy, and
who by reason of the spare Time they had, in their almost idle
Employment, had most leisure to make Verses, and to be in Love;
without somewhat of which Passion, no *Opera* can possibly subsist.

'Tis almost needless to speak any thing of that noble Language,
in which this Musical *Drama* was first invented and perform'd. All,
who are conversant in the *Italian*, cannot but observe, that it is
the softest, the sweetest, the most harmonious, not only of any
modern Tongue, but even beyond any of the Learned. It seems
indeed to have been invented for the sake of Poetry and Musick;
the Vowels are so abounding in all Words, especially in the Terminations.

nations of them, that excepting some few Monosyllables, the whole Language ends in them. Then the Pronunciation is so Manly, and so Sonorous, that their very Speaking has more of Musick in it than *Dutch Poetry*, and *Song*. It has withal deriv'd so much Copiousness and Eloquence from the *Greek* and *Latin*, in the Composition of Words, and the Formation of them, that (if after all we must call it Barbarous) 'tis the most Beautiful and most Learned of any Barbarism in Modern Tongues. And we may, at least, as justly praise it, as *Pyrrhus* did the *Roman* Discipline and Martial Order, that it was of *Barbarians*, (for so the *Greeks* call'd all other Nations,) but had nothing in it of Barbarity. This Language has in a manner been refin'd and purify'd from the *Gothick*, ever since the time of *Dante*; which is above Four Hundred Years ago; and the *French*, who now cast a longing Eye to their Country, are not less ambitious to possess their Elegance in Poetry and Musick; in both which they labour at Impossibilities. 'Tis true indeed, they have reform'd their Tongue, and brought both their Prose and Poetry to a Standard; the Sweetness, as well as the Purity is much improv'd, by throwing off the unnecessary Consonants, which made their Spelling tedious, and their Pronunciation harsh: But after all, as nothing can be improv'd beyond its own *Species*, or farther than its original Nature will allow; as an ill Voice, though never so throughly instructed in the Rules of Musick, can never be brought to sing harmoniously, nor many an honest Critick ever arrive to be a good Poet; so neither can the natural Harshness of the *French*, or their perpetual ill Accent, ever refin'd into perfect Harmony like the *Italian*. The *English* has yet more natural Disadvantages than the *French*; our original *Teutonick* consisting most in Monosyllables, and those incumbred with Consonants, cannot possibly be freed from those Inconveniences. The rest of our Words, which are deriv'd from the *Latin* chiefly, and the *French*, with some small Sprinklings of *Greek*, *Italian* and *Spanish*, are some Relief in Poetry, and help us to soften our uncouth Numbers; which together with our *English Genius*, incomparably beyond the trifling of the *French*, in all the nobler Parts of Verse, will justly give us the Preheminence. But, on the other hand, the Effeminacy of our Pronunciation, (a Defect common to us, and to the *Danes*,) and our Scarcity of Female Rhimes, have left the Advantage of Musical Composition for Songs, though not for Recitative, to our Neighbours.

Through

Through thefe Difficulties, I have made a fhift to ftruggle, in my part of the performance of this *Opera*; which, as mean as it is, deferves at leaft a Pardon, becaufe it has attempted a Difcovery beyond any former Undertaker of our Nation; only remember, that if there be no North-Eaft Paffage to be found, the Fault is in Nature, and not in me. Or, as *Ben. Johnfon* tells us in the *Alchymiff*, when Projection had fail'd, and the Glaffes were all broken, there was enough however in the Bottoms of them to cure the Itch; fo I may thus be pofitive, That if I have not fucceeded, as I defire, yet there is fomewhat ftill remaining, to fatisfie the Curiofity or Itch of Sight and Hearing. Yet I have no great reafon to defpair; for I may without vanity, own fome Advantages, which are not. common to every Writer; fuch as are the knowledge of the *Italian* and *French* Language, and the being converfant with fome of their beft Performances in this kind; which have furnifh'd me with fuch variety of Meafures, as have given the Compofer Monfieur *Grabut* what Occafions he cou'd wifh, to fhew his extraordinary Talent, in diverfifying the Recitative, the Lyrical Part, and the Chorus: In all which, (not to attribute any thing to my own Opinion,) the beft Judges, and thofe too of the beft Quality, who have honour'd his Rehearfals with their Prefence, have no lefs commended the Happinefs of his Genius than his Skill. And let me have the Liberty to add one thing; that he has fo exactly exprefs'd my Senfe, in all Places, where I intended to move the Paffions, that he feems to have enter'd into my Thoughts, and to have been the Poet as well as the Compofer. This I fay, not to flatter him, but to do him Right; becaufe amongft fome *Englifh* Muficians, and their Scholars, (who are fure to judge after them,) the imputation of being a *French-man*, is enough to make a Party, who malicioufly endeavour to decry him. But the knowledge of *Latin* and *Italian* Poets,. both which he poffeffes, befides his Skill in Mufick, and his being acquainted with all the Performances of the *French Opera's*, adding to thefe the good Senfe to which he is born, having rais'd him to a degree above any Man, who fhall pretend to be his Rival on our Stage. When any of our Countrey-men excell him, I fhall be glad, for the fake of old *England*, to be fhewn my Errour; in the mean time, let Vertue be commended, though in the Perfon of a Stranger.

If I thought it convenient, I cou'd here difcover fome Rules which I have given to my felf in writing of an *Opera* in general;

and of this *Opera* in particular : But I confider,that the Effect would only be,to have my own performance meafur'd by the Laws I gave; and confequently to fet up fome little Judges, who not underftanding throughly, wou'd be fure to fall upon the Faults, and not to acknowledge any of the Beauties; (an hard meafure which I have often found from falfe Criticks.) Here therefore, if they will Criticize, they fhall do it out of their own *Fond*; but let them be firft affur'd,that their Ears are nice ;·for their is neither writing nor judging on this Subject, without that good quality. 'Tis no eafie Matter in our Language to make Words fo fmooth, and Numbers fo harmonious, that they fhall almoft fet themfelves, and yet there are Rules for this in Nature: and as great a certainty of Quantity in our Syllables, as either in the *Greek* or *Latin* : But let Poets and Judges underftand thofe firft, and then let them begin to ftudy *Englifh*. When they have chaw'd a while upon thefe Preliminaries, it may be they will fcarce adventure to tax me with want of Thought, and Elevation of Fancy in this Work; for they will foon be fatisfied, That thofe are not of the nature of this fort of Writing : The neceffity of double Rhimes, and ordering of the Words and Numbers for the fweetnefs of the Voice, are the main Hinges on which an *Opera* muft move ; and both of thefe are without the compafs of any Art to teach another to perform;unlefs Nature in the firft place has done her part, by enduing the Poet with that nicety of hearing, that the Difcord of Sounds in Words fhall as much offend him, as a Seventh in Mufick wou'd a good Compofer. I have therefore no need to make Excufes for Meannefs of Thought in many places: The *Italians*, with all the Advantages of their Language, are continually forc'd upon it ; or rather they affect it. The chief Secret is in the choice of Words ; and by this Choice I do not here mean Elegancy of Expreffion ; but Propriety of Sound, to be varied according to the Nature of the Subject. Perhaps a time may come, when I may treat of this more largely, out of fome Obfervations which I have made from *Homer* and *Virgil*, who amongft all the Poets, only underftood the Art of Numbers, and of that which was properly call'd *Rithmus* by the Ancients.

The fame Reafons which deprefs Thought in an *Opera*, have a ftronger Effect upon the Words ; efpecially in our Language : For there is no maintaining the Purity of *Englifh* in fhort Meafures, where the Rhime returns fo quick, and is fo often Female, or double Rhime, which is not natural to our Tongue, becaufe it confifts too much of Monosyllables, and those too, most commonly clogg'd with Consonants; for which reason I am often forc'd to Coin new Words, revive some that are antiquated, and botch others; as if I had not serv'd out my Time in Poetry, but was bound 'Prentice to some Doggrel Rhimer, who makes Songs to Tunes, and sings them for a Livelihood. 'Tis true, I have not been often put to this Drudgery; but where I have, the Words will sufficiently shew, that I was then a Slave to the Composition, which I will never be again: 'Tis my part to Invent, and the Musician's to Humour that Invention. I may be counsell'd, and will always follow my Friend's Advice, where I find it reasonable; but will never part with the Power of the *Militia*.

I am now to acquaint my Reader with somewhat more particular concerning this *Opera*, after having begg'd his Pardon for so long a Preface to so short a Work. It was originally intended only for a Prologue to a Play, of the Nature of the *Tempest*; which is a Tragedy mix'd with *Opera*; or a *Drama* written in blank Verse, adorn'd with Scenes, Machines, Songs and Dances: So that the Fable of it is all spoken and acted by the best of the Comedians; the other part of the Entertainment to be perform'd by the same Singers and Dancers who are introduc'd in this present *Opera*. It cannot properly be call'd a Play, because the Action of it is suppos'd to be conducted sometimes by supernatural Means, or Magick; nor an *Opera*, because the Story of it is not sung. But more of this at its proper time: But some intervening Accidents having hitherto deferr'd the performance of the main Design, I propos'd to the Actors, to turn the intended Prologue into an Entertainment by it self, as you now see it, by adding two Acts more to what I had already written. The Subject of it is wholly Allegorical; and the Allegory it self so very obvious, that it will no sooner be read than understood. 'Tis divided according to the plain and natural Method of every Action, into Three Parts. For even *Aristotle* himself is contented to say simply, That in all Actions there is a Beginning, a Middle, and an End; after which Model, all the *Spanish* Plays are built.

The Descriptions of the Scenes, and other Decorations of the Stage, I had from Mr. *Betterton*, who has spar'd neither for Industry, nor Cost, to make this Entertainment perfect, nor for Invention of the Ornaments to beautifie it.

B To

To conclude, Though the Enemies of the Compoſer are not few, and that there is a Party form'd againſt him, of his own Profeſſion, I hope, and am perſuaded, that this Prejudice will turn in the end to his Advantage. For the greateſt part of an Audience is always unintereſs'd, though ſeldom knowing; and if the Muſick be well compos'd, and well perform'd, they who find themſelves pleas'd, will be ſo wiſe as not to be impos'd upon, and fool'd out of their ſatisfaction. The newneſs of the Undertaking is all the hazard: When *Opera's* were firſt ſet up in *France*, they were not follow'd over eagerly; but they gain'd daily upon their Hearers, till they grew to that height of Reputation, which they now enjoy. The *Engliſh* I confeſs, are not altogether ſo Muſical as the *French*; and yet they have been pleas'd already with the *Tempeſt*, and ſome Pieces that follow'd, which were neither much better Written, nor ſo well compos'd as this. If it finds encouragement, I dare pro-miſe my ſelf to mend my Hand, by making a more pleaſing Fable: In the mean time, every Loyal *Engliſhman* cannot but be ſatisfy'd with the Moral of this, which ſo plainly repreſents the double Reſtoration of his Sacred Majeſty.

POST-SCRIPT.

THis *Preface being wholly Written before the Death of my late. Royal Maſter,* (quem ſemper acerbum, ſemper honoratum, ſic Dii voluiſtis, habebo,) *I have now, lately reveiw'd it, as ſuppo-ſing I ſhou'd find many Notions in it, that wou'd require correction on coo-ler Thoughts. After Four Months lying by me, I look'd on it as no lon-ger mine, becauſe I had wholly forgotten it; but, I confeſs, with ſome ſatisfaction, and perhaps a little Vanity, that I found my ſelf enter-tain'd by it; my own Judgment was new to me, and pleas'd me when I look'd on it as another Man's: I ſee no Opinion that I wou'd re-tract or alter, unleſs it be, that poſſibly the* Italians *went not ſo far as* Spain, *for the Invention of their* Opera's. *They might have it in their own Country; and that by gathering up the Shipwrecks of the* Athenian *and* Roman *Theatres; which we know were adorn'd with Scenes, Muſick, Dances and Machines, eſpecially the* Grecian. *But of this the Learned Monſieur* Voſſius, *who has made our Nation his ſecond Country, is the beſt, and perhaps the only Judge now living:*
As

The Preface.

As for the Opera *it felf, it was all compos'd, and was juſt ready to have been perform'd, when he, in Honour of whom it was principally made, was taken from us.*

He had been pleas'd twice or thrice to command, that it ſhou'd be practiſ'd before him, eſpecially the Firſt and Third Acts of it; and publickly declar'd more than once, That the Compoſition and Chorus's were more Juſt, and more Beautiful, than any he had heard in England. *How nice an Ear he had in Muſick, is ſufficiently known; his Praiſe therefore has eſtabliſh'd the Reputation of it, above Cenſure, and made it in a manner Sacred. 'Tis therefore humbly and religiouſly dedicated to his Memory.*

It might reaſonably have been expected, that his Death muſt have chang'd the whole Fabrick of the Opera; *or at leaſt a great part of it. But the Deſign of it originally was ſo happy, that it needed no alteration, properly ſo call'd; for the Addition of Twenty or Thirty Lines in the Apotheoſis of* Albion, *has made it entirely of a Piece. This was the only way which cou'd have been invented, to ſave it from a Botch'd Ending; and it fell luckily into my Imagination: As if there were a kind of Fatality, even in the moſt trivial things concerning the Succeſſion; a Change was made, and not for the worſe, without the leaſt confuſion or diſturbance: And thoſe very Cauſes which ſeem'd to threaten us with Troubles, conſpir'd to produce our laſting Happineſs.*

Names

Names of the Persons, Represented in the same Order as they appear first upon the STAGE.

Mercury.	*Nereids.*
Augusta. London.	*Acacia. Innocence.*
Thamesis.	*Tyranny.*
Democracy.	*Asebia. Atheism, or Ungodliness.*
Zelota, Feign'd Zeal.	*Proteus.*
Archon. The General.	*Venus.*
Juno.	*Fame.*
Iris.	*A Chorus of Cities.*
Albion.	*A Chorus of Rivers.*
Albanius.	*A Chorus of the People.*
Pluto.	*A Chorus of Furies.*
Alecto.	*A Chorus of Nereids and Tritons.*
Apollo.	*A Grand Chorus of Hero's, Loves, and*
Neptune.	*Graces.*

The

The FRONTISPIECE.

THE *Curtain rises, and a new Frontispiece is seen, joyn'd to the great Pylasters, which are on each side of the Stage: On the Flat of each Basis is a Shield, adorn'd with* Gold: *In the middle of the Shield on one side, are two Hearts, a small Scrowl of Gold over 'em, and an Imperial Crown over the Scrowl; on the other, in the Shield are two Quivers full of Arrows Saltyre,* &c. *Upon each Basis stands a Figure bigger than the Life; one represents Peace, with a Palm in one, and an Olive-Branch in the other hand; t'other Plenty, holding a* Cornucopia, *and resting on a Pillar. Behind these Figures are large Columns of the* Corinthian *Order, adorn'd with Fruit and Flowers: Over one of the Figures on the Trees is the King's Cypher, over the other, the Queen's: Over the Capitals, on the Cornice, sits a Figure on each side; one presents* Poetry, *crown'd with Laurel, holding a Scrowl in one Hand, the other with a Pen in it, and resting on a Book; the other,* Painting, *with a Pallat and Pencils,* &c. *On the Sweep of the Arch lies one of the Muses, playing on a Base Voyal; another of the Muses, on the other side, holding a Trumpet in one Hand, and the other on a Harp. Between these Figures, in the middle of the Sweep of the Arch, is a very large Pannel in a Frame of Gold; in this Pannel is painted on one side a Woman representing the City of* London, *leaning her Head on her Hand in a dejected posture, (shewing her Sorrow and Penitence for her Offences;) the other Hand holds the Arms of the City, and a Mace lying under it: On the other side, is a Figure of the* Thames, *with his Legs shackl'd, and leaning on an empty Urn: Behind these, are Two Imperial Figures; one representing His present Majesty;*

Majesty ; *and the other the Queen* : *By the King stands* Pallas, *(or Wisdom and Valour,) holding a* Charter *for the City, the King extending his Hand, as raising her drooping Head, and restoring her to her ancient Honour and Glory* : *Over the City are the envious devouring* Harpies *flying from the Face of Majesty* : *By the Queen stand the* Three Graces, *holding Garlands of Flowers, and at her Feet* Cupids *bound, with their Bows and Arrows broken, the Queen pointing with her Scepter to the River, and commanding the Graces to take off their Fetters. Over the King, in a Scrowl, is this Verse of* Virgil,

Discite Justitiam, moniti, & non temnere Divos.

Over the Queen, this of the same Author,

Non ignara mali, miseris succurrere disco.

ALBION

ALBION,

AND

ALBANIUS;

An Opera.

Decorations of the Stage in the Firſt Act.

TE Curtain riſes, and there appears on either ſide of
the Stage, next to the Frontiſpiece, a Statue on Horſe-
back of Gold, on Pedeſtals of Marble, enrich'd with
Gold, and bearing the Imperial Arms of England . One of theſe
Statues is taken from that of the late King, at Charing-Croſs ;
the other, from that Figure of his preſent Majeſty (done by that
noble Artiſt Mr. Gibbons) at Windſor.

The Scene, is a Street of Palaces, which lead to the Front of
the Royal Exchange ; the great Arch is open, and the view is
continued through the open part of the Exchange, to the Arch on
the other ſide, and thence to as much of the Street beyond, as
could properly be taken.

Mercury

Mercury defcends in a Chariot drawn by Ravens.

He comes to Augufta, *and* Thamefis. *They lie on Cou-ches, at a diftance from each other in dejected poftures; She at-tended by Cities, He by Rivers.*

Onthe fide of Augufta's *Couch are Painted Towers falling, a Scarlet Gown, and Gold Chain, a Cap of Maintenance thrown down, and a Sword in a Velvet Scabbard thruft through it, the City Arms, a Mace with an old ufelefs Charter, and all in difor-der. Before* Thamefis *are broken ;Reeds, Bull-rufhes, Sedge,* &c. *with his Urn Reverft.*

A C T. I.

Mercury *Defcends.*

Merc. **T**Hou glorious Fabrick ! ftand for ever, ftand:
Well Worthy Thou to entertain
The God of Traffick, and of Gain,
To draw the Concourfe of the Land,
And Wealth of all the Main.
But where the Shoals of Merchants meeting ?
Welcome to their Friends repeating,
Bufie Bargains deafer found!
Tongues Confus'd of every Nation ?
Nothing here but Defolation,
Mournful filence reigns around.
 Aug. O *Hermes !* pity me !
I was, while Heav'n did fmile,
The Queen of all this Ifle,
Europe's Pride,
And *Albion's* Bride ;
But gone my Plighted Lord ! ah, gone is He !
O *Hermes !* pity me !

         Tham.

Tham. And I the Noble Flood, whose tributary Tide
Does on her Silver Margent smoothly glide ;
But Heav'n grew jealous of our happy state :
And bid revolving Fate,
Our Doom decree ;
No more the King of Floods am I,   } *These two Lines are sung by Re-*
No more the Queen of *Albion,* She! } *prises, betwixt* Aug.& Tham.
   Aug. O *Hermes !* pity me! } *Sung by* Augusta *and* Thamesis
   Tham. O *Hermes !* pity me ! } *together.*
   Aug. Behold !
   Tham. Behold !
   Aug. My Turret's on the ground
That once my Temples crown'd !
   Tham. The Sedgy Honours of my Brow's dispers'd !
My Urn revers'd !
   Merc. Rise, rise, *Augusta,* rise !
And wipe thy weeping Eyes :
Augusta ! for I call thee so !
'Tis lawful for the Gods to know
Thy future Name,
And growing Fame.
Rise, rise, *Augusta,* rise.
   Aug. O never, never will I rise!
Never will I cease my mourning,
Never wipe my weeping Eyes,
Till my plighted Lord's returning!
Never, never will I rise !
   Merc. What brought Thee, Wretch, to this Despair ?
The Cause of thy Misfortune show.
   Aug. It seems the Gods take little Care
Of Humane Things below,
When even our Suffrings here they do not know!
   Merc. Not unknowing came I down,
Disloyal Town !
Speak ! didst not Thou
Forsake thy Faith, and break thy Nuptial Vow ?
   Aug. Ah 'tis too true ! too true !
But what cou'd I, unthinking City, do?
Faction sway'd me,
Zeal allur'd me,

C   Both

Both affur'd me,
Both betray'd me!

Merc. Suppofe me fent
Thy *Albion* to reftore,
Can'ft thou repent?

Aug. My Falfhood I deplore!

Tham. Thou feeft her mourn; and I.
With all my Waters, will her Tears fupply.

Merc. Then by fome Loyal Deed regain
Thy long loft Reputation,
To wafh away the Stain
That blots a Noble Nation!
And free thy famous Town again
From Force of Ufurpation.

Chor. } We'll wafh away the ftain
of all. } That blots a noble Nation.
And free this famous Town again
From force of Ufurpation.   [*Dance of the Followers of* Mercury.

Aug. Behold *Democracy* and *Zeal* appear;
She that allur'd my Heart away,
And He that after made a Prey.

Merc. Refift, and do not fear!

Chorus of all.] Refift, and do not fear!   [*Enter* Democracy *and* Zeal
attended *by* Archon.

Democ. Nymph of the City! bring thy Treafures,
Bring me more
To wafte in Pleafures.

Aug. Thou haft exhaufted all my Store,
And I can give no more.

Zeal. Thou Horny Flood, for *Zeal* provide
A new Supply; And fwell thy Moony Tide,
That on thy buxom Back the floating Gold may glide.

Tham. Not all the Gold the Southern Sun produces,
Or Treafures of the fam'd *Levant*,
Suffice for Pious Ufes,
To feed the facred hunger of a Saint!

Democ. Woe to the Vanquifh'd, woe!
Slave as thou art,
Thy Wealth impart,
And me thy Victor know!

Zeal

Zeal. And me thy Victor know,
Refiftlefs Arms are in my hand,
Thy Barrs fhall burft at my Command,
Thy Towry Head lye low.
Woe to the Vanquifh'd, woe !
  Aug. Were I not bound by Fate
For ever, ever here,
My Walls I would tranflate
To fome more happy Sphere,
Remov'd from fervile fear.
  Tham. Remov'd from fervile fear,
Wou'd I could difappear
And fink below the Mayn ;
For Common-wealth's a Load
My old Imperial Flood
Shall never never bear again.

A Common-wealth's a Load   } *Thamefis and* Augufta *toge-*
Our old Imperial Flood   *ther.*
Shall never never never bear again. }
  Dem. Pull down her Gates, Expofe her bare ;
I muft enjoy the proud, difdainful Fair.
Hafte, *Archon,* Hafte
To lay her wafte !
  Zeal. I'll hold her faft
To be embrac'd !
  Dem. And fhe fhall fee
A Thoufand Tyrants are in thee,
A Thoufand Thoufand more in me!
Archon } From the *Caledonian* Shore
  to *Aug.* } Hither am I come to fave thee,
Not to force or to enflave thee,
But thy *Albion* to reftore :
Hark ! the Peals the People ring.
Peace and Freedom and a King.
  Chor.] Hark ! the Peals the People ring,
Peace, and Freedom, and a King.
  Aug. Tham. to Arms ! to Arms!
  Archon. I lead the way !
  Merc. Ceafe your Alarms !

And

And stay, brave *Archon*, stay!
'Tis Doom'd by Fates Decree!
'Tis Doom'd that *Albion*'s Dwelling,
All other Isles excelling,
By Peace shall Happy be!
  Archon. What then remains for me?.
  Merc. Take my *Caduceus*! Take this awful Wand,
With this th'Infernal Ghosts I can command,
And strike a Terrour thro' the *Stygian* Land.
Common-wealth will want Pretences,
Sleep will creep on all his Senses;
Zeal that lent him her Assistance, Archon *touches* Democracy.
Stand amaz'd without Resistance. *with a Wand.*
  Dem. I feel a lazy Slumber lays me down!
Let *Albion*! let him take the Crown!
Happy let him reign,
Till I wake again!   [*falls asleep.*
  Zeal. In vain I rage, In vain,
I rouze my Powers;
But I shall wake again;
I shall to better Hours.
Ev'n in Slumber I will vex him;
Still perplex him,
Still incumber:
Know you that have ador'd him,
And Sovereign Power afford him,
We'll reap the Gains
Of all your Pains,
And seem to have restor'd him!

                        [*Zel. falls asleep.*

  Aug. and *Tham.* A stupifying sadness
Leaves Her without motion;
But Sleep will cure her Madness.
And cool her to Devotion.

*A double Pedeftal rifes: On the Front of it is painted in Stone-Co-
lour, Two Women ; One holding a double-fac'd Vizor ; the other
a Book, reprefenting* Hypocrifie *and* Phanaticifm ; *when*
Archon *has charmed* Demacracy *and* Zeal *with the Caduceus of* Mercury, *they fall afleep on the Pedeftal, and
it finks with them.*

Merc. CEafe, *Augufta !* Ceafe thy Mourning,.
    Happy Days appear,
God like *Albion* is returning
Loyal Hearts to Chear !
Every Grace his Youth adorning,
Glorious as the Star of Morning,
Or the Planet of the Year.
    Chor. God-like *Albion* is returning, *&c.*
    Merc. to ⎱ Hafte away, Loyal Chief, hafte away.
    Arch. ⎰ No Delay, but obey :
To receive thy Lov'd Lord! hafte away.   [*Exit* Arch..
    Tham. Medway and *Ifis*, you that augment me,
Tides that encreafe my Watry Store,
And you that are Friends to Peace and Plenty,.
    Send my Merry Boys all afhore ;
Sea-Men Skipping,
Mariners Leaping,
Shouting Tripping,
Send my Merry Boys all afhore !.

A Dance of Water-men in the King's *and* Duke's *Liveries:*

The Clouds divide, and Juno *appears in a Machine drawn by Peacocks; while a Symphony is playing, it moves gently forward, and as it descends, it opens and discovers the Tail of the Peacock, which is so large, that it almost fills the opening of the Stage between Scene and Scene.*

Merc. THE Clouds divide, what Wonders,
     What Wonders do I see!
The Wife of *Jove*! Tis She,
That Thunders, more than Thundring He!
   Juno, No, *Herme,* No;
'Tis Peace above
As 'tis below:
For *Jove* has left his wandring Love.
   Tham. Great Queen of gathering Clouds;
Whose Moisture fills our Floods,
See; we fall before Thee,
Prostrate we adore Thee!
   Aug. Great Queen of Nuptial Rites,
Whose Pow'r the Souls unites,
And fills the Genial Bed with chaste Delights
See; we fall before Thee,
Prostrate we adore Thee!
   Juno. 'Tis ratify'd above by every God,
And *Jove* has firm'd it with an Awful Nod;
That *Albion* shall his Love renew:
But oh, ungrateful Fair,
Repeated Crimes-beware,
And to his Bed be true!

Iris

Iris appears on a very large Machine. This was really seen the 18th. of March 1684. by Capt. Christopher Gunman, on Board his R. H. Yacht, then in Calais Pierre : He drew it as it then appear'd, and gave a Draught of it to us. We have only added the Cloud where the Person of Iris sits.

Juno. Speak *Iris*, from *Batavia*, speak the News !
Has she perform'd my dread Command,
Returning *Albion* to his longing Land,
Or dares the Nymph refuse ?

Iris. *Albion*, by the Nymph attended,
Was to *Neptune* recommended,
Peace and Plenty spread the Sails :
Venus in her Shell before him,
From the Sands in Safety bore him,
And supply'd *Etesian* Gales.   [*Retornella.*
Archon on the Shore commanding,
Lowly met him at his Landing,
Crowds of People swarm'd around ;
Welcome rang like Peals of Thunder ;
Welcome, rent the Skies asunder ;
Welcome, Heav'n and Earth resound.

Juno. Why stay we then on Earth
When Mortals laugh and love ?
'Tis time to mount above
And send *Astræa* down,
The Ruler of his Birth,
And Guardian of his Crown.
'Tis time to mount above,
And send *Astræa* down.

Me. Ju. Ir. 'Tis time to mount above,
And send *Astræa* down.   [Mer. Ju. *and* Iris *ascend.*

Aug. and *Tham.* The Royal Squadron marches,
Erect Triumphal Arches,
For *Albion* and *Albanius* :
Rejoyce at their returning,
The Passages adorning :
The Royal Sqadron marches,
Erect Triumphal Arches ·
For *Albion* and *Albanius.*

                                        Part

Part of the Scene disappears, and the Four Triumphal Arches ere-Eted at His Majesties Coronation are seen.

Albion appears, Albanius by his Side, preceded by Archon, followed by a Train, &c.

Full HAil, Royal *Albion*, Hail.
Chor.   *Aug.* Hail Royal *Albion*. Hail to thee,
Thy longing Peoples Expectation :
   Tham. Sent from the God's to set us free
from Bondage and from Usurpation !
   Aug. To pardon and to pity me,
And to forgive a guilty Nation !
   Tham. Behold the differing Climes agree,
Rejoycing in thy Restauration.

Entry. Representing the Four Parts of the World, rejoycing at the Restauration of Albion.

ACT II.

The Scene is a Poetical Hell. The Change is Total. *The Upper Part of the Houſe, as well as the Side Scenes. There is the Figure of* Prometheus *chain'd to a Rock, the Vulture gnawing his Liver.* Siſiphus *rowling the Stone, the* Belides, *&c. beyond, abundance of Figures in various Torments. Then a great Arch of Fire. Behind this three Pyramids of Flames in perpetual Agitation. Beyond this; glowing Fire, which terminates the Proſpeꝏ.*

Pluto, *the Furies;* with Alecto, Democracy and Zelota.

Plut. INfernal Offspring of the Night,
  Debarr'd of Heav'n your Native Right,
  And from the glorious Fields of Light,
Condemn'd in Shades to drag the Chain,
And fill with groans the gloomy Plain ;
Since Pleaſures here are none below,
Be Ill our Good, our Joy be Woe ;
Our Work t'embroil the Worlds above,
Diſturb their Union, diſunite their Love,
And blaſt the Beauteous Frame of our Victorious Foe.
Democ. & *Ze-* ⎰ Oh thou for whom thoſe Worlds are made,
 lot. together. ⎱ Thou Sire of all things and their end,
From hence they ſpring, and when they fade,
In ſhuffled Heaps they hither tend;
Here Humane Souls receive their Breath,
And wait for Bodies after Death.
 Dem. Hear our Complaint, and grant our Pray'r.

D

Pluto. Speak what you are,
And whence you fell ?

Democ. I am thy firſt begotten Care,
Conceiv'd in Heav'n ; but born in Hell,
When Thou didſt bravely undertake in fight
Yon Arbitrary Pow'r,
That rules by Sovereign Might,
To ſet thy Heav'n-born Fellows free
And leave no difference in Degree,
In that Auſpicious Hour
Was I begot by Thee.

Zelota. One Mother bore us at a Birth,
Her Name was *Zeal* before ſhe fell ;
No fairer Nymph, in Heav'n or Earth,
Till Saintſhip taught her to rebel:
But looſing Fame,
And changing Name,
She's now the *Good Old Cauſe* in Hell.

Plut. Dear Pledges of a Flame not yet forgot,
Say, what on Earth has been your Lot ?

Dem. & Zel. The Wealth of *Albion's* Iſle was ours,
Auguſta ſtoop'd with all her ſtately Tow'rs !

Dem. *Democracy* kept Nobles under.

Zel. *Zeal* from the Pulpit roar'd like Thunder.

Dem. I trampled on the State.

Zel. I Lorded o'er the Gown.

Dem. & Zel. We both in Triumph ſate
Uſurpers of the Crown.
But oh prodigious Turn of Fate !
Heaven controuling,
Sent us rowling, rowling, down.

Plut. I wonder'd how of late our Acherontick Shore
Grew thin, and Hell unpeopl'd of her Store ;
Charon, for want of Uſe, forgot his Oar.
The Souls of Bodies Dead flew all ſublime,
And hither none return'd to purge a Crime :
But now I ſee ſince *Albion* is reſtor'd,
Death has no Buſ'neſs, nor the vengeful Sword.
'Tis too too much that here I lye
From glorious Empire hurl'd ;

By

By *Jove* excluded from the Sky,
By *Albion* from the World.

Dem. Were Common-Wealth reftor'd again,
Thou fhould'ft have Millions of the flain
To fill thy dark Abode.

Zel. For He a Race of Rebels fends,
And *Zeal* the Path of Heav'n pretends ;
But ftill miftakes the Rode.

Pluto. My lab'ring Thought
At length hath wrought
A bravely bold Defign,
In which you both fhall joyn ;
In borrow'd Shapes to Earth return ;
Thou *Commonwealth,* a Patriot feem,
Thou *Zeal,* like true Religion burn,
To gain the giddy Crowd's Efteem.
Aletto, thou to fair *Augufta* go,
And all thy Snakes into her Bofom throw.

Dem. Spare fome to fling
Where they may fting
The Breaft of *Albion's* King.

Zel. Let Jealoufies fo well be mix'd,
That great *Albanius* be unfix'd !

Pluto. Forbear your vain Attempts, forbear ;
Hell can have no admittance there :
The Peopfes Fear will ferve as well,
Make him fufpected, them rebel.

Zel. Y'have all forgot
To forge a Plot
In feeming Care of *Albion's* Life ;
Infpire the Croud
With Clamours loud
T'involve his Brother and his Wife.

Aletto. Take of a Thoufand Souls at thy Command,
The bafeft, blackeft of the Stygian Band:
One that will fwear to all they can invent,
So throughly Damn'd that he can ne'er repent :
One often fent to Earth,
And ftill at every Birth

He took a deeper ftain :
One that in *Adam's* time was *Cain :*
One that was burnt in *Sodom's* Flame,
For Crimes ev'n here too black to name :
One, who through every form of ill has run :
One, who in *Naboth's* days, was *Belial's* Son :
One, who has gain'd a Body fit for Sin;
Where all his Crimes
Of former Times
Lie crowded in a Skin.
    Pluto. Take him ;
Make him
What you pleafe ;
For He
Can be
A Rogue with eafe.
One for mighty Mifchief born :
He can Swear and be Forfworn.
Pluto and *Alecto* ⎱Take him, make him what you pleafe ;
  take him, *&c.* ⎰For he can be a Rogue with eafe.
    Pluto. Let us laugh, let us laugh, let us laugh at our Woes,
The Wretch that is damn'd has nothing to lofe.
Ye Furies advance
With the *Ghofts* in a Dance,
'Tis a Jubilee when the World is in Trouble.
When People rebel
We frolick in Hell ;
But when the King falls, the Pleafure is double :

                                      ⎱ *A fingle Entry of a*
                                        ⎰ *Devil follow'd by an*
                                        Entry of 12 *Devils.*

    Chorus. Let us laugh, let us laugh, let us laugh at our Woes,
The Wretch that is damn'd hath nothing to lofe.

The Scene changes to a Prospect taken from the middle of the
Thames; *one side of it begins at* York-Stairs, *thence to*
White-Hall, *and the* Mill-Bank, &c. *The other from*
the Saw-Mill, *thence to the* Bishops Palace, *and on as far*
as can be seen in a clear Day.

Enter Augusta; *She has a Snake in her Bosom, hanging down.*

Aug. O Jealousie, thou raging Ill,
    Why hast thou found a Room in Lovers Hearts,
Afflicting what thou canst not kill,
And poysoning Love himself, with his own Darts?
I find my *Albion's* Heart is gone,
My first Offences yet remain,
Nor can Repentance Love regain;
One writ in Sand, alas, in Marble one.
I rave, I rave, my Spirits boyl
Like Flames increas'd, and mounting high with pouring Oyl:
Disdain and Love succeed by turns;
One freezes me, and t'other burns; It burns.
Away soft Love, thou Foe to rest,
Give Hate the full Possession of my Breast.
Hate is the nobler Passion far
When Love is ill repay'd;
For at one Blow it ends the War,
And cures the Love-sick Maid.

Enter Democracy *and* Zelota; *one represents a* Patriot, *the*
other Religion.

Dem. LEt not thy generous Passion waste its Rage,
    But once again restore our Golden Age;
Still to weep and to complain,
Does but more provoke Disdain.
Let Publick Good
Inflame thy Blood;

With

With Crowds of Warlike People thou art ftor'd,
And heaps of Gold ;
Reject thy old,
And to thy Bed receive another Lord.

   Zel. Religion fhall thy Bonds releafe,
For Heav'n can loofe, as well as tie all ;
And when 'tis for the Nation's peace
A King is but a King on Tryal ;
When Love is loft, let Marriage end,
And leave a Hufband for a Friend.

   Dem. With Jealoufie fwarming
The People are Arming
And frights of Oppreflion invade them

   Zelot. If they fall to relenting,
for fear of repenting,
Religion fhall help to perfuade 'em.

   Aug. No more, no more Temptations ufe
To bend my Will ;
How hard a Task 'tis to refufe
A pleafing Ill ?

   Dem. Maintain the feeming duty of a Wife,
A modeft fhow will jealous Eyes deceive,
Affect a fear for hated *Albion*'s Life,
And for imaginary Dangers grieve.

   Zelot. His Foes already ftand protected,
His Friends by publick Fame fufpected,
Albanius muft forfake his Ifle :
A Plot contriv'd in happy hour
Bereaves him of his Royal Pow'r,
For Heav'n to mourn and Hell to fmile.

The former Scene continues.

Enter Albion and Al-
banius with a Train.

THen Zeal and Common-wealth infeft
   My Land again ;
The fumes of madnefs that poffeft
The Peoples giddy Brain,

Once

Once more difturb the Nation's reft,
And dye Rebellion in a deeper Stain.

2.

Will they at length awake the fleeping Sword,
And force revenge from their offended Lord ?
How long, ye Gods, how long
Can Royal Patience bear
Th' Infults and Wrong
Of mad Men's jealoufies, and caufelefs fear ?

3.

I thought their love by mildnefs might be gain'd,
By Peace I was reftor'd, in Peace I reign'd :
But Tumults, Seditions,
And haughty Petitions,
Are all the effects of a merciful Nature ;
Forgiving and granting,
E'er Mortals are wanting,
But leads to Rebelling againft their Creator.

Mercury *defcends.*

Merc. With pity *Jove* beholds thy State,
But *Jove* is circumfcrib'd by Fate;
Th' o'erwhelming Tide rowls on fo faft,
It gains upon this Iflands waft :
And is oppos'd too late ! too late !
    Albion. What then muft helplefs *Albion* do ?
    Merc. Delude the fury of the Foe,
And to preferve *Albanius,* let him go ;
For 'tis decreed,
Thy Land muft bleed,
For Crimes not thine, by wrathful *Jove* ;
A Sacred Flood
Of Royal Blood,
Cries Vengeance, Vengeance loud above.

Mercury

Mercury ascends.

Albion. Shall I, t' aſſwage
Their Brutal rage,
The Regal Stem deſtroy ;
Or muſt I loſe,
(To pleaſe my Foes,)
My ſole remaining joy ?
Ye Gods what worſe,
What greater Curſe,
Can all your Wrath employ ?
 Alban. Oh *Albion* ! hear the Gods and me !
Well, am I loſt in ſaving Thee.
Not exile or danger can fright a brave Spirit
With Innocence guarded,
With Vertue rewarded ;
I make of my ſufferings a Merit.
 Albion. Since then the Gods, and Thou wilt have it ſo ;
Go : (can I live once more to bid Thee ?) go,
Where thy Misfortunes call Thee and thy Fate :
Go, guiltleſs Victim of a guilty State,
In War my Champion to defend,
In peaceful Hours, when Souls unbend,
My Brother, and what's more my Friend !
Born where the Foamy Billows roar,
On *Seas* leſs dang'rous than the Shore :
Go, where the Gods thy Refuge have aſſign'd :
Go from my ſight ; but never from my Mind.
 Alban. Whatever Hoſpitable Ground
Shall be for me, unhappy Exile, found,
Till Heav'n vouchſafe to ſmile ;
What Land ſo e'er,
Tho none ſo dear,
As this ungrateful Iſle ;
O think ! O think ! no diſtance can remove
My vow'd Allegiance, and my loyal Love.
 Albion. and *Alban.* The Roſie finger'd Morn appears,
And from her Mantle ſhakes her Tears,

In promife of a glorious Day :
The Sun, returning, Mortals chears,
And drives the Rifing Mifts away,
In promife of a glorious Day.   (*Ritornelle.*

---

*The farther part of the Heaven opens and difcovers a Machine ;
as it moves forwards the Clouds which are before it divide, and
fhew the Perfon of* Apollo, *holding the Reins in his hand. As
they fall lower, the Horfes appear with the Rays and a great
Glory about* Apollo.

Apoll. ALL Hail ye Royal pair !
The God's peculiar care :
Fear not the Malice of your Foes ;
Their dark defigning
And combining,
Time and Truth fhall once expofe :
Fear not the Malice of your Foes.

2.

My facred Oracles affure,
The Tempeft fhall not long indure ;
But when the Nation's Crimes are purg'd away,
Then fhall you both in Glory fhine ; ⎫
Propitious both, and both Divine :   ⎬ Apollo *goes forward out*
In Luftre equal to the God of Day.   ⎭ *of fight.*

Neptune *rifes out of the Water, and a Train of Rivers,* Tritons, *and Sea-Nymphs attend him.*

Thames. OLd Father Ocean calls my Tyde :
Come away, come away ;
The Barks upon the Billows ride,
The Mafter will not ftay ;

E   The

The merry Bofon from his fide,
His Whiftle takes to check and chide
The lingring Lads delay,
And all the Crew aloud has cry'd,
Come away, come away.

See the God of Seas attends Thee,
Nymphs Divine, a Beauteous Train :
All the calmer Gales befriend Thee
In thy paffage o'er the Main :
Every Maid her Locks is binding,
Every *Triton*'s Horn is winding,
Welcome to the watry Plain.

Chacon.

Two *Nymphs* and Triton *fuig.*

YE Nymphs, the Charge is Royal,
　　Which you muft convey ;
Your Hearts and Hands employ all,
　　Haften to obey ;
When Earth is grown difloyal,
Shew there's Honour in the Sea.
The Chacon *continues.*
The Chorus of Nymphs and Tritons *repeat the fame Verfes.*
The Chacon *continues.*
Two Nymphs and Tritons.

Sports and Pleafures fhall attend you
　　Through all the Watry Plains,
　　Where *Neptune* Reigns:
Venus ready to defend you,
　　And her Nymphs to eafe your Pains.
　　No ftorm fhall offend you,
　　　Paffing the Main ;
Nor Billow threat in vain,
　　So Sacred a Train,

Till

Till the Gods that defend you,
    Reftore you again.
        The Chacon *continues.*
The Chorus repeat the fame Verfes, Sports and Pleafure, *&c.*
        The Chacon *continues.*
    The two Nymphs and Triton *Sing.*

See at your bleft returning
    Rage difappears ;
The Widow'd Ifle in Mourning
    Dries up her Tears,
With Flowers the Meads adorning
    Pleafure appears,
And love difpels the Nations caufelefs fears.
        The Chacon *continues.*
The Chorus of Nymphs and Triton *repeat the fame Verfes,* See at
    your bleft returning, *&c.*
        The Chacon *continues.*
Then the Chorus repeat. See the God of Seas, *&c. And this Chorus*
    concludes the Act.

A C T. III.

    The Scene is a view of Dover, *taken from the Sea : a row of
Cliffs fill up each fide of the Stage, and the Sea the middle of it,
which runs into the* Peer : *beyond the* Peer, *is the Town of* Dover : *on each fide of the Town, is feen a very high Hill ; on one
of which is the Caftle of* Dover ; *on the other, the great Stone
which they call the* Devils drop. *Behind the Town feveral Hills
are feen at a great diftance which finifh the view.*

    Enter Albion *bare-headed :* Acacia *or* Innocence *with him.*

Albion. Behold ye Powers! from whom I own
    A Birth immortal, and a Throne :
        E 2

                              Se

See a Sacred King uncrown'd,
See your Offspring, *Albion*, bound :
The Gifts you gave with lavifh hand,
Are all beftow'd in vain :
Extended Empire on the Land,
Unbounded o'er the Main.

Acacia.

Empire o'er the Land and Main,
Heav'n that gave can take again ;
But a mind that's truly brave,
Stands defpifing,
Storms arifing,
And can ne'er be made a Slave.
   Albion. Unhelp'd I am, who pity'd the diftrefs'd,
And none oppreffing, am by all opprefs'd ;
Betray'd, forfaken, and of hope bereft :
   Acacia. Yet ftill the Gods and Innocence are left.
   Albion. Ah ! what eanft thou avail.
Againft Rebellion arm'd with Zeal,
And fac'd with Publick Good ?
O Monarchs fee
Your Fate in me !
To rule by Love,
To fhed no Blood,
May be extoll'd above ;
But here below,
Let Princes know
'Tis fatal to be good.
   Chorus of both. To rule by Love, &c.
   Acacia. Your Father *Neptune* from the Seas,
Has *Nereids* and blue *Triton's* fent,
To charm your Difcontent.

Nereids

Nereids *rife out of the Sea and fing*, Tritons *dance.*

FRom the low Palace of old Father Ocean,
    come we in pity your Cares to deplore :
Sea-racing Dolphins are train'd for our Motion,
Moony Tides fwelling to rowl us a-fhore.

2.

Ev'ry Nymph of the Flood, her Treffes rending,
Throws off her Armlet of Pearl in the Main ;
Neptune in anguifh his Charge unattending,]
Veffels are foundring, and Vows are in vain.

Enter Tyranny, Democracy, *reprefented by* Men, *attended by*
Afebia, Zelota, *Women.*

Tyran. HA, ha, 'tis what fo long I wifh'd and vow'd,
    Our Plots and Delufions,
Have wrought fuch Confufions,
That the Monarch's a Slave to the Croud.
  Democ. A Defign we fomented,
  Tyr. By Hell it was new !
  Dem. A falfe Plot invented,
  Tyr. To cover a true.
  Democ. Firft with promis'd Faith we flatter'd,
  Tyr. Then Jealoufies and Fears we fcatter'd.
  Afebia. We never valu'd right and wrong,
But as they ferv'd our Caufe ;
  Zelot. Our Bufinefs was to pleafe the Throng;
And court their wild applaufe :
  Afebia. For this we brib'd the Lawyers Tongue,
And then deftroy'd the Laws.
  Chor. For this, &c.
  Tyran. To make him fafe; we made his Friends our Prey ;
  Dem. To make him great we fcorn'd his Royel Sway,
  Tyran. And to confirm his Crown, we took his Heir away.

Dem.

Democ. T'encreafe his ftore,
We kept him poor :
   Tyran. And when to wants we had betray'd him,
To keep him low,
. Pronounc'd a Foe,
· Who e'er prefum'd to aid him.
   Afebia. But you forget the nobleft part,
And Mafter-piece of all your Art,
You told him he was fick at Heart.   }
   Zelot. And when you could not work belief
In *Albion* of th' imagin'd Grief ;
Your perjur'd vouchers in a Breath,
·Made Oath that he was fick to Death ;
And then five hundred Quacks of Skill
: Refolv'd 'twas fit he fhould be ilL
   Afebia. Now heigh for a Common-wealth,
· We merrily Drink and Sing,
'Tis to the Nation's Health,
: For every Man's a King.
   Zelot. Then let the Mask begin,
.The *Saints* advance,
To fill the Dance,
·And the Property Boys comes in.

The Boys in White begin a Fantaftick Dance

   Chor. Let the Saints afcend the Throne.
   Dem. Saints have Wives, and Wives have Preachers,
Guifted Men, and able Teachers ;
Thefe to get, and thofe to own ;
   Chor. Let the Saints afcend the Throne.

   Afebia. Freedom is a bait alluring ;
.Them betraying, us fecuring,
While to Soverign Pow'r we foar.
   Zelota. Old Delufions new repeated,
Shews them born but to be cheated,
As their Fathers were before.

Six

Six Sectaries begin a formal affected Dance, the two gravest whisper the other Four, and draw 'em into the Plot: They pull out and deliver Libels to them, which they receive.

Democr. SEE Friendless *Albion* there alone,
    Without Defence
But Innocence;
Albanius now is gone.
  Tyran. Say then, What must be done?
  Dem. The Gods have put him in our hand.
  Zelota. He must be slain!
  Tyran. But who shall then Command?
  Dem. The People: for the Right returns to those,
Who did the Trust impose.
  Tyran. 'Tis fit another Sun shou'd rise,
To cheer the World, and light the Skies.
  Dem. But when the Sun,
His race has run,
And neither cheers the World, nor lights the Skies;
'Tis fit a Common-wealth of Stars shou'd rise.
  Asebia. Each noble Vice,
Shall bear a Price,
And Vertue shall a Drug become:
An empty Name
Was all her Fame,
But now she shall be Dumb.

  Zelota. If open Vice be what you drive at,
A Name so broad we'll ne'er connive at.
Saints love Vice, but more refin'dly,
Keep her close, and use her kindly.
  Tyran. Fall on.
  Dem. Fall on: E'er *Albion's* Death we'll try,
If one or many shall his room supply.

The white Boys dance about the Saints : The Saints draw out the Aſſociation, and offer it to them : They refuſe it and quarrel about it : Then the white Boys and Saints fall into a confus'd Dance, imitating fighting. The white Boys at the end of the Dance, being driven out by the Sectaries with Proteſtant Flails.

Albion. SEE the Gods my Cauſe defending,
When all humane help was paſt !
Acacia. Factions mutually contending,
By each other fall at laſt.
Albion. But is not yonder *Proteus* Cave,
Below that Steep,
Which riſing Billows brave ?
Acacia. It is : And in it lies the God aſleep :
And ſnorting by,
We may deſcry,
The Monſters of the Deep.
Albion. He knows the paſt,
And can reſolve the future too.
Acacia. 'Tis true !
But hold him faſt,
For he can change his Hew.

The Cave of Proteus *riſes out of the Sea, it conſiſts of ſeveral Arches of Rock-work, adorn'd with Mother of Pearl, Coral, and abundance of Shells of various kinds : Thro' the Arches is ſeen the Sea, and parts of* Dover-Peer *: In the middle of the Cave is* Proteus *aſleep on a Rock adorn'd with Shells, &c. Like the Cave.* Albion *and* Acacia *ſeize on him ; and while a Symphony is playing, he ſinks as they are bringing him forward, and changes himſelf into a Lyon, a Crocodile, a Dragon, and then to his own ſhape again : He comes toward the front of the Stage, and Sings.*

Symphony.

Proteus. ALbion, lov'd of Gods and Men,
Prince of Peace too mildly Reigning

Ceaſe

Ceafe thy Sorrow and complaining ;
Thou fhalt be reftor'd agen :
Albion, lov'd of Gods and Men.

2.

Still thou art the Care of Heav'n,
In thy Youth to Exile driv'n :
Heav'n thy ruin then prevented,
Till the guilty Land repented :
In thy Age, when none could aid Thee,
Foes confpir'd, and Friends betray'd Thee ;
To the brink of Danger driv'n,
Still thou art the Care of Heav'n.
    Albion. To whom fhall I my Prefervation owe ?
    Proteus. Ask me no more ! for 'tis by *Neptune*'s Foe.

Proteus defcends.

Democracy *and* Zelota *return with their Faction.*

    Democ. Our feeming Friends, who join'd alone,
To pull down one, and build another Throne,
Are all difpers'd and gone :
We brave republick Souls remain.
    Zelot. And 'tis by us that *Albion* muft be Slain :
Say, whom fhall we employ
The Tyrant to deftroy ?
    Democ. That Archer is by Fate defign'd,
With one Eye clear, and t'other blind.
    Zelota. He feems infpir'd to do't.
    Omnes. Shoot Holy *Cyclop*, fhoot.

The one Ey'd Archer advances, the reft follow : A Fire arifes
    betwixt them and Albion.   [*Ritornel.*

    Democ. Lo ! Heav'n and Earth combine,
To blaft our bold Defign.

F   What

What Miracles are fhown?
Nature's alarm'd,
And Fires are arm'd,
To guard the Sacred Throne.
 Zelota. What help, when jarring Elements confpire
To punifh our audacious Crimes.
Retreat betimes,
To fhun th' avenging Fire.
 Chor. To fhun the avenging Fire.   [*Ritor.*

As they are going back a Fire arifes from behind: They all fink together.

 Albion. Let our tuneful Accents upwards move,
Till they reach the vaulted Arch of thofe above ;
Let us adore 'em ;
Let us fall before 'em :
 Acacia. Kings they made, and Kings they love.
When they protect a rightful Monarch's Reign,
The Gods in Heav'n, the Gods on Earth maintain.
 Both. When they protect, &c.
 Albion. But fee what Glories guild the Main.
 Acacia. Bright *Venus* brings *Albanius* back again,
With all the Loves and Graces in her Train.

A Machine rifes out of the Sea : It opens and difcovers Venus *and* Albanius *fitting in a great Scallop-fhell, richly adorn'd :* Venus *is attended by the Loves and Graces,* Albanius *by* Heroes. *The Shell is drawn by Dolphins : It moves forward, while a Simphony of Fluts-Doux, &c. is playing till it Lands 'em on the Stage, and then it clofes and finks.*

Venus Sings.

ALbion, Hail ; The Gods prefent Thee,
 All the richeft of their Treafures,
Peace and Pleafures,

        To

To content Thee,   } *Graces and Loves,*
Dancing their eternal Meafures.   } *Dance an Entry.*

Venus. But above all humane Bleſſing ;
Take a Warlike Loyal Brother,
Never Prince had ſuch another :
Conduct, Courage, Truth expreſſing,   } *Here the Heroes*
All Heroick Worth poſſeſſing.   } *Dance is performed.*
    Chor. of all. But above all, &c.   [*Ritor.*

Whilſt a Symphony is playing ; a very large, and a very glorious
  Machine deſcends : The figure of it Oval, all the Clouds ſhi-
  ning with Gold, abundance of Angels and Cherubins flying a-
  bout 'em, and playing in 'em ; in the midſt of it ſits Apollo
  on a Throne of Gold : he comes from the Machine to Albion.

    Phœb. From *Jove's* Imperial Court,
Where all the Gods reſort ;
In awful Council met,
Surprizing News I bear :
Albion the Great,
Muſt change his Seat,
For He's adopted there.
    Ven. What Stars above ſhall we diſplace ?
Where ſhall he fill a Room Divine ?
    Nept. Deſcended from the Sea God's Race,
Let him by my *Orion* ſhine.
    Phœb. No, Not by that tempeſtuous Sign :
Betwixt the *Balance* and the *Maid,*
The Juſt,
Auguſt,
And peaceful Shade,
Shall ſhine in Heav'n with Beams diſplay'd,
While great *Albanius* is on Earth obey'd :
    Ven. Albanius Lord of Land and Main,
Shall with fraternal Vertues Reign ;

       .   And

And add his own,
To fill the Throne;
Ador'd and fear'd, and lov'd no lefs:
In War Victorious, mild in Peace,
The Joy of Men, and *Jove's* increafe.

Acacia. O Thou! Who mount'ft th'Æthereal Throne,
Be kind and happy to thy own;
Now *Albion* is come,
The People of the Sky,
Run gazing and cry,
Make Room, make Room,
Make Room for our New Deity.

Here Albion *mounts the Machine, which moves upward flowly.*

A full Chorus of all that Acacia *fung.*

Ven. Behold what Triumphs are prepar'd to grace
Thy glorious Race,
Where Love and Honour claim an equal place;
Already they are fix'd by Fate,
And only ripening Ages wait.

The Scene changes to a walk of very high Trees: At the end of the Walk is a view of that part of Windfor, *which faces* Eaton: *In the midft of it is a row of fmall Trees, which lead to the Caftle-hill : In the firft Scene, part of the Town and part of the Hill : In the next the Terrace Walk, the King's Lodgings, and the upper part of* St. George's Chappel, *then the Keep ; and laftly, that part of the Caftle, beyond the Keep.*

In the Air is a Vifion of the Honours of the Garter ; the Knights in Proceffion, and the King under a Canopy : Beyond this, the upper end of St. George's Hall.

Fame rifes out of the middle of the Stage, ftanding on a Globe ; on which is the Arms of England : *The Globe refts on a Pedeftal: On the Front of the Pedeftal is drawn a Man with a long, lean, pale Face, with Fiends Wings, and Snakes twifted round his Body: He is incompafs'd by feveral Phanatical Rebellious Heads, who fuck Poifon from him, which runs out of a Tap in his Side.*

Fame.

Fame. R Enown, affume thy Trumpet!
From Pole to Pole refounding :
Great *Albion's* Name ;
Great *Albion's* Name fhall be
The Theme of Fame, fhall be great *Albion's* Name,
Great *Albion's* Name, Great *Albion's* Name.
Record the Garters Glory :
A Badge for Heroes, and for Kings to bear :
For Kings to bear !
And fwell th'Immortal Story,
With Songs of Gods, and fit for Gods to hear ;
And fwell th'Immortal Story,
With Songs of Gods, and fit for Gods to hear ;
For Gods to hear.

A full Chorus of all the Voices and Instruments: Trumpets and Ho-Boys make Ritornelloes of all Fame sings ; and Twenty four Dancers are all the time in a Chorus, and Dance to the end of the Opera.

F I N I S.

PROLOGUE
To the O P E R A.

By Mr. Dryden.

FUll twenty years and more, our lab'ring Stage
   Has loſt, on this incorrigible Age :
Our Poets, the John Ketches of the Nation,
Have ſeem'd to laſh ye, ev'n to Excoriation :
But ſtill no ſign remains ; which plainly notes,
You bore like Heroes, or you brib'd like Oates.
What can we do, when mimicking a Fop,
Like beating Nut-trees, makes a larger Crop ?
Faith we'll e'en ſpare our Pains ; and to content you,
Will fairly leave you what your Maker meant you.
Satyre was once your Phyſick, Wit your Food ;
One nouriſh'd not, and t'other drew no Blood.
We now preſcribe, like Doctors in Deſpair,
The Diet your weak Appetites can bear.
Since hearty Beef and Mutton will not do,
Here's Julep dance, Ptiſan of Song and Show :
Give you ſtrong Senſe, the Liquor is too heady ;
You're come to Farce, that's Aſſes Milk, already
Some hopeful Youths there are, of callow Wit,
Who one day may be Men, if Heav'n think fit ;
Sound may ſerve ſuch, e'er they to Senſe are grown ;
Like Leading-ſtrings, till they can walk alone .
But yet to keep our Friend in Count'nance, know,
The Wiſe Italians firſt invented Show ;
Thence, into France the Noble Pageant paſt ;
'Tis England s Credit to be cozen'd laſt.

Free-

Freedom and Zeal have chous'd you o'er and o'er ;
'Pray' give us leave to bubble you once more ;
You never were so cheaply fool'd before ;
We bring you Change, to humour your Disease ;
Change for the worse has ever us'd to please :
Then 'tis the Mode *of* France, *without whose Rules,*
None must presume to set up here for Fools :
In France, *the oldest Man is always young,*
See Operaes *daily, learns the Tunes so long,*
Till Foot, Hand, Head, keep time with ev'ry Song.
Each sings his part, eccboing from Pit and Box,
With his hoarse Voice, half Harmony, half Pox.
Le plus grand Roy du Monde, *is always ringing ;*
They show themselves good Subjects by their singing.
On that condition, set up every Throat ;
You Whigs may sing, for you have chang'd your Note.
Cits and Citesses, raise a joyful strain,
'Tis a good Omen to begin a Reign :
Voices may help your Charter to restoring,
And get by singing, what you lost by roaring.

EPILOGUE
To the OPERA.

By Mr. Dryden.

AFter our Esop's Fable shown to day,
    I come to give the Moral of the Play.
Feign'd Zeal, you saw, set out the speedier pace ;
But, the last Heat, Plain Dealing *won the Race :*
Plain Dealing *for a Jewel has been known ;*
But ne'er till now the Jewell of a Crown.

                                   When

When Heav'n made Man, to show the Work Divine,
Truth was his Image, stamp'd upon the Coin :
And, when a King is to a God refin'd,
On all he says and does, he stamps his Mind :
This proves a Soul without allay, and pure ;
Kings, like their Gold, should every touch endure.
To dare in Fields is Valour ; but how few
Dare be so throughly Valiant to be true ?
The Name of Great, let other Kings affect :
He's Great indeed, the Prince that is direct.
His Subjects know him now, and trust him more,
Than all their Kings, and all their Laws before.
What safety could their publick Acts afford ?
Those he can break ; but cannot break his Word.
So great a Trust to him alone was due ;
Well have they trusted whom so well they knew.
The Saint, who walk'd on Waves, securely trod,
While he believ'd the beckning of his God ;
But, when his Faith no longer bore him out,
Began to sink, as he began to doubt.
Let us our native Character maintain,
'Tis of our growth, to be sincerely plain.
T' excel in Truth, we Loyally may strive ;
Set Privilege against Prerogative :
He plights his Faith, and we believe him Just ;
His Honour is to promise, ours to trust,
Thus Britain's Basis on a Word is laid,
As by a Word the World it self was made.

www.ingramcontent.com/pod-product-compliance
Lightning Source LLC
Chambersburg PA
CBHW032120080426
42733CB00008B/997